How to Leverage Business Credit to Fund Real Estate Purchases

A Step-by-Step Guide to Funding Real Estate Deals Without Using Personal Credit or Cash

By Joe Correa

Published by Live Stronger Faster

This book is for educational and informational purposes only. The author and publisher are not engaged in rendering legal, financial, or other professional advice. Readers should consult a qualified professional before making any financial decisions.

First Edition

Table of Contents

Introduction

Welcome to *How to Leverage Business Credit to Fund Real Estate Purchases*. If you've ever dreamed of owning property but felt limited by your personal credit or lack of capital, this book is for you.

Over the next few chapters, you'll learn how to use business credit—completely separate from your personal credit—to secure funding for real estate investments. You'll discover how to build business credit profiles, access high-limit business credit cards and lines of credit, and strategically position yourself to qualify for business real estate loans.

Whether you're a first-time investor or an entrepreneur looking to expand your portfolio, this guide will help you understand how to control assets using credit that's not tied to your personal finances. And the best part? It's legal, scalable, and doable from anywhere.

Let's get started on your journey from credit to capital—one property at a time.

Chapter 1: Why Business Credit is a Game Changer for Real Estate

If you've ever tried to purchase real estate using your personal credit, you've likely faced some combination of the following: debt-to-income ratio limits, personal liability, hard credit pulls, and the emotional weight of tying up your name and finances in a high-risk investment. That's not just frustrating—it's limiting. The more real estate you try to buy, the more those limitations tighten around you like a vice.

That's where business credit comes in. Business credit doesn't just open new doors; it opens entirely new buildings—quite literally. It gives you access to funding that's not reported on your personal credit, allows you to separate your risk, and builds your business into a funding magnet for real estate opportunities that others can't touch.

But before we get into how to build and leverage business credit, let's talk about why it changes the game entirely for real estate investors like you.

The Personal Credit Trap

Imagine this scenario: You buy a single-family rental using a conventional mortgage tied to your personal credit. That mortgage shows up on your personal credit report, which affects your utilization and your debt-to-income ratio. Then you try to buy a second property, and suddenly lenders see you as higher risk—even if that first property is cash flowing and profitable.

This is one of the main frustrations for aspiring investors. They want to grow a portfolio, but personal credit limits how far and how fast they can go.

Now contrast that with someone using business credit. That same property—if financed through business credit lines or loans—would not show up on their personal credit report. This means they could continue building their business credit profile and qualify for more capital without it ever interfering with their personal score or credit capacity.

That's not just smarter—it's scalable.

Business Credit is Not Just for Corporations

Many people assume business credit is only for big companies or enterprises with employees, huge revenue, and long operating histories. That's false. You can start building business credit with a brand-new LLC or corporation—even as a solopreneur with zero revenue.

Lenders and vendors who report to commercial credit bureaus look at how your business is set up, whether you've established a credible foundation, and how you manage the credit you're given. In fact, many of the starter vendors we'll talk about in later chapters will extend net-30 terms to brand-new businesses without requiring personal guarantees.

And as you build those accounts and pay on time, you create a strong business credit profile that opens the door to higher-limit credit cards, lines of credit, and real estate-friendly funding tools like DSCR loans.

You don't need a huge business—you just need a properly set up business.

Real Estate Investors Who Use Business Credit Win Bigger

Let's take two real estate investors: Sarah and James.

Sarah is using her personal credit to fund everything. Her first rental was financed with a conventional loan under her name. Her credit score dropped slightly because of the new debt. Her DTI increased. And when she applied for a second loan, she had to jump through hoops to prove she could handle both mortgages.

Now take James. He formed an LLC, built a business credit profile, and got approved for a $50,000 business line of credit. He used that line of credit as a down payment for a fixer-upper duplex and financed the rest with a DSCR loan under his LLC.

The property doesn't affect his personal credit. He didn't use his own money. And now he has a cash-flowing asset that increases his business creditworthiness for the next deal.

James can rinse and repeat. Sarah hits a wall.

Why Lenders Prefer Lending to Businesses

Here's a secret many new investors don't know: lenders actually prefer lending to businesses in many cases. Businesses can deduct interest. They can show higher income. They can separate assets. And when structured correctly, they pose less liability for the lender in terms of collections and asset recovery.

More importantly, lending to businesses is scalable. A business can take on multiple properties without the same constraints personal borrowers face. And businesses often seek more expensive, income-generating properties, which equals bigger deals and more profits for lenders.

That's why many lenders offer specialized products like business credit cards, working capital lines, DSCR mortgages, commercial loans, and SBA-backed financing—all of which can be used to fund or refinance real estate deals.

Real Leverage Comes From Separation

One of the most powerful aspects of using business credit for real estate is asset protection. When you buy real estate under your personal name and finance it with personal credit, you're liable. If someone sues, if the deal goes bad, or if you default, your name is on the line.

With business credit, and a property held under an LLC or corporation, you separate yourself from the asset. If structured and operated properly, that LLC takes on the debt, not you personally. You get the upside—cash flow, appreciation, tax advantages—while minimizing downside risk.

That separation is the foundation of real wealth. The wealthiest investors don't own everything under their personal name. They control assets through entities, funded by strategic credit, and protected by proper structures.

And it all starts with understanding how business credit works.

You're Not Just an Investor. You're a Funding Strategist.

If you walk away from this chapter with just one insight, let it be this: You're not just buying houses. You're building a business. You're leveraging capital. You're growing net worth by mastering the game of funding.

Think of real estate like a board game. Everyone's on the board trying to buy properties, collect rent, and increase their wealth. Some people play using personal money and credit, which limits the number of moves they can make. Others use business credit and financing strategies that give them more turns, more options, and more leverage.

The person with the most access to smart capital wins.

So if you've ever felt stuck because you didn't have the cash, or your credit wasn't perfect, or the banks said no—now you know. There's another way.

In the chapters ahead, I'll show you exactly how to build your business credit from scratch, unlock the right funding tools, and use them to buy real estate without relying on your personal credit. We'll talk about lenders, vendors, DSCR loans, credit stacking, and even exit strategies.

But before we do any of that, we need to start at the root: building the right foundation for your business credit.

That's what we'll cover next.

Chapter 2: Setting Up the Foundation for Business Credit

Before you can start leveraging business credit for real estate purchases, you need a rock-solid foundation. Think of your business like a house: you wouldn't build on sand, and you wouldn't finance property with a business that looks untrustworthy to lenders. This chapter is about getting everything in place so banks, credit bureaus, and vendors see you as a serious, fundable business.

We'll cover:

1. Choosing the right legal structure
2. Registering your business correctly
3. Creating a credible online and offline presence
4. Opening business banking and vendor accounts
5. Avoiding red flags that kill your creditworthiness

Follow each step closely, and you'll be ready to build real, usable credit fast.

Step 1: Choose the Right Legal Structure

To build business credit, your company must be a **separate legal entity**. That means:

- **Sole proprietors** do *not* qualify. Business credit built under your own name is tied to your personal Social Security number.
- You must form an **LLC (Limited Liability Company)** or a **Corporation (S-Corp or C-Corp)**.

LLCs are ideal for real estate investors. They're simple to create, flexible for taxes, and offer liability protection. Corporations work well for more complex business setups but come with more requirements.

Action Step: Register your LLC or corporation with your state's Division of Corporations. Make sure the business name is professional and ideally includes a neutral or finance-related term (e.g., "ClearPoint Acquisitions LLC" instead of "Joe Buys Houses Fast").

Step 2: Obtain Your EIN and Business Licenses

An **EIN (Employer Identification Number)** is like a Social Security number for your business. You'll use it to open bank accounts, file taxes, and apply for credit.

Action Step:

- Go to the IRS website and apply for your EIN online. It's free and instant.

Next, get any **local business licenses** required by your city or county. Even if you operate online, many jurisdictions require a business tax receipt or occupational license.

Why this matters: Lenders and credit bureaus cross-check your information. If anything is inconsistent or missing—like your EIN, licensing, or business address—your applications may be denied or flagged.

Step 3: Create a Fundable Business Profile

Lenders do online research. If your business can't be found—or what they find looks unprofessional—they assume you're high-risk. Here's how to fix that.

You need the following:

- A **dedicated business phone number** (can be a virtual service like Grasshopper or RingCentral)
- A **professional business email** (e.g., info@YourBusiness.com—not Gmail or Yahoo)
- A **real business address** (not a P.O. Box; virtual office addresses are okay if they meet lender requirements)
- A **simple website** that describes your services and contact info
- Your business listed on **Google My Business**, Yelp, and online directories

Action Step:

- Register your business on Google Maps.
- Set up your website with a domain matching your business name.
- Use a clean, modern layout and include basic pages: Home, About, Services, and Contact.

Pro Tip: Make sure your business name, address, and phone number are consistent *everywhere*. This includes your website, bank accounts, licenses, utility bills, and credit applications.

Step 4: Open a Business Bank Account

This step is required before you can apply for credit—and it shows you're operating as a real business. You'll also need your business bank account to receive funds, make payments, and track expenses for real estate purchases.

Action Step:

- Choose a bank that reports to business credit bureaus (e.g., Bank of America, Chase, Wells Fargo).
- Take your Articles of Organization, EIN, and business license to open the account.
- Deposit at least $100 to start.
- Never co-mingle personal and business funds. That's a legal and tax disaster waiting to happen.

Bonus Tip: Ask your banker about future credit products (lines of credit, credit cards, etc.) and what they look for. Starting a relationship early helps you qualify faster.

Step 5: Apply for a D-U-N-S Number

The **D-U-N-S Number** is issued by Dun & Bradstreet (D&B), one of the major business credit reporting bureaus. It's required to build your credit file and apply for funding with many lenders and vendors.

Action Step:

- Go to DNB.com and apply for a D-U-N-S Number. It's free.
- Register your business and verify your information.
- You'll receive your number within 1–2 weeks.

Why it matters: This is how D&B starts tracking your business credit. No D-U-N-S = no report = no credit score.

Step 6: Get Net-30 Vendor Accounts

"Net-30" vendors give you products or services with 30 days to pay. These accounts often report to business credit bureaus—helping you establish your first trade lines.

Top starter vendors:

- **Uline.com** – office and warehouse supplies

- **Grainger.com** – tools and industrial supplies
- **Quill.com** – office and cleaning products
- **Summa Office Supplies** – office goods with easy approvals
- **Nav.com** – credit monitoring that reports to D&B and Experian

Action Step:

- Apply for 3–5 of these accounts.
- Order small amounts and pay on time or early.
- Use your business name, EIN, business address, and bank info—no personal credit check required.

Pro Tip: Wait 30–60 days and then check your business credit reports. You'll start seeing trade lines appear, and your credit score will begin forming.

Step 7: Avoid These Common Fundability Killers

Many businesses never get approved for funding because of small, preventable mistakes. Avoid these:

- **P.O. Box as business address** – Most lenders reject it
- **Using a personal email (like Gmail)** – Looks unprofessional

- **No online presence** – Lenders can't verify your legitimacy
- **Inconsistent business info across platforms** – Raises red flags
- **Applying for credit too early** – Wait until you have 3–5 reporting accounts
- **Mixing personal and business finances** – Violates tax and legal rules

Remember: You are *creating the perception* of a stable, fundable business. Appearances matter as much as operations when it comes to credit approvals.

Final Checklist Before Moving Forward

Here's your business credit foundation checklist. Make sure each box is checked before proceeding:

- Formed LLC or Corporation
- Obtained EIN from IRS
- Secured required business licenses
- Set up a professional website and email
- Got a business phone number and physical address
- Opened a business bank account

- Registered with Dun & Bradstreet and received D-U-N-S
- Opened and used 3–5 Net-30 vendor accounts

Once you've completed these steps, you'll be ready to move to the next level—**building real business credit** that you can use to finance your real estate deals without personal guarantees or high interest rates.

In the next chapter, we'll talk about how to build your business credit profile the right way—from tier 1 to tier 3 vendors—and how to strategically qualify for high-limit credit cards and lines of credit.

Let's keep building.

From Hustler to CEO — Maya's Foundation

Maya sat at her kitchen table in a one-bedroom apartment in Phoenix, Arizona. Her laptop was open, not for browsing listings on Zillow like usual, but because today marked the day she was officially done hustling in the dark. For the past three years, she had been wholesaling properties—flipping contracts to investors—always using her personal cell phone, her Gmail, and her own name on every deal. She had closed a few good flips, made some decent money, but she always felt like she was stuck at the bottom of the ladder. Scraping by. Starting from scratch every time.

It hit her hardest when she tried to buy her first rental property. She was ready to scale—but the bank didn't see her as a business. They saw her as a freelancer with fluctuating income, no business assets, and a maxed-out credit card she'd been using to cover deal costs.

She was done playing small.

That morning, she poured her coffee and typed into Google: "How to build business credit for real estate." She didn't know what would come next—but she knew something had to change.

The Shift: Legitimizing the Hustle

She read for hours and found stories of other investors who built real estate portfolios by separating their personal finances from their business. They used LLCs, business credit, and DSCR loans. Maya had always thought she needed a perfect credit score or a big chunk of cash to get started. Turns out, what she really needed was structure.

That day, she registered "Keystone Acquisitions LLC" with the Arizona Corporation Commission. It cost her $85 and took less than an hour. It was surreal—finally seeing her business have a name, a structure, and a legal standing. This wasn't just a side hustle anymore. This was real.

By lunchtime, she applied for her EIN through the IRS website—free and instant. She opened a document to organize her new identity: business name, EIN, phone number, and a list of to-dos. She felt like a new version of herself. Focused. Confident.

Building a Fundable Identity

She quickly realized that just forming an LLC wasn't enough. To get funding, lenders had to see her business as legitimate. That meant no Gmail address, no P.O. Box, no random cash apps for payments. She set up a business email using her new domain, keystoneacquisitions.com, and ordered a virtual business address from a verified commercial provider downtown.

Then came the business phone line. For $29/month, she got a toll-free number routed to her cell. Now, when lenders called, she answered like a CEO—not like someone winging it from her living room.

She spent the next few days building a simple but clean website: "Helping Arizonans Sell Fast While We Build Stronger Communities." It had her story, her services, and a photo of her smiling in front of a property she helped renovate. It wasn't fancy—but it made her proud. It made her real.

The Bank Visit That Changed Everything

Two weeks later, she walked into a Chase Bank wearing her best blazer and a folder of her business documents. She had everything they needed: her Articles of Organization, her EIN letter, her new business address, and a $1,000 check to deposit.

"I'd like to open a business checking account," she said.

The banker smiled and walked her through the process. As they talked, Maya asked, "What kind of credit products do you offer for new businesses?"

The banker leaned in, impressed. "Most people don't ask that, but we do have a business credit card program and a line of credit option once your account is in good standing."

She left the branch with a business debit card, a printed checkbook with her LLC's name on it, and—most importantly—a foot in the door.

That night, she stared at her new check. *Pay to the order of: Keystone Acquisitions LLC.* She teared up a little. Not from sentimentality, but from clarity. This wasn't just an account—it was leverage.

Laying the First Bricks of Credit

With her business bank account open, Maya moved on to trade credit. She had read about Net-30 vendors—companies that give you 30 days to pay after you order, and more importantly, report to credit bureaus. She applied for Uline, Quill, and Grainger using only her EIN and business info.

At first, she ordered small: $60 in shipping supplies from Uline. A $40 pack of toner from Quill. Nothing major, but just enough to get her foot in the credit door. She paid them off early, tracked her payments, and followed up with each vendor to confirm that they reported to D&B.

She also applied for her D-U-N-S number and began monitoring her credit profile through Nav. Within 30 days, she started seeing trade lines appear under her business. Her Paydex score—the business version of a FICO—was born.

She was building her business's reputation the same way she had built her own: piece by piece, deal by deal.

The Confidence of Separation

One day, she got a call from a seller looking to unload a duplex. The numbers worked. The area was solid. And for the first time, Maya didn't panic about where she'd get the money.

Instead, she looked at her business checking balance. She looked at her credit lines. She called a DSCR lender she'd been researching and said, "Hi, I'm Maya from Keystone Acquisitions. We're interested in financing a buy-and-hold property under our company."

They didn't ask about her personal credit. They asked about the property's cash flow and her business bank statements. That deal ended up being her first true business-funded purchase.

It cash-flowed $500/month per unit. It appreciated within six months. And it built the confidence she never had when operating from her personal accounts.

Maya's story is real. Not because she's extraordinary—but because she chose to treat her business *like a business.*

You don't need perfect credit. You don't need a huge savings account. You need a strong foundation. An entity. An identity. A structure that lenders can trust and money can flow through.

Like Maya, the first step toward funding your real estate dreams is taking yourself seriously enough to build it right from the ground up.

Chapter 3: Building Your Business Credit Profile from Scratch

Now that your business foundation is solid—your LLC is formed, your business bank account is active, and you've established a professional presence—it's time to **build your actual business credit profile**.

This chapter will guide you step-by-step through:

1. Understanding business credit reporting agencies
2. Establishing your first tradelines
3. Creating a tiered credit-building plan (Tier 1 to Tier 3)
4. Monitoring your business credit
5. Optimizing your profile for faster access to higher limits

Step 1: Know the Business Credit Reporting Agencies

There are **three main credit bureaus** that track and score your business:

- **Dun & Bradstreet (D&B)**: Known for the Paydex score (0–100 scale). A score of 80+ indicates you pay on time or early.
- **Experian Business**: Provides an Intelliscore (1–100). 76+ is low risk.

- **Equifax Small Business**: Tracks business payment history and credit utilization.

Each bureau has different vendors reporting to them, so your strategy should include accounts that report to all three when possible.

Action Step:

- Register for a free Nav account (nav.com) to monitor your business credit scores and track tradeline reporting.

Step 2: Start with Tier 1 Net-30 Vendors

Tier 1 vendors are companies that:

- Approve brand-new businesses without requiring a personal guarantee
- Report to D&B, Experian, or Equifax
- Extend Net-30 terms (payment due in 30 days)

Top Tier 1 Vendors:

1. **Uline.com** – Reports to D&B. Office and shipping supplies.
2. **Quill.com** – Reports to D&B and Experian. Office supplies.

3. **Grainger.com** – Reports to D&B and Equifax. Industrial tools.
4. **Summa Office Supplies** – Reports to Equifax.
5. **Nav.com** – Monthly credit reporting subscription.

How to Apply:

- Use your EIN—not your SSN
- Ensure your business info matches your EIN, bank account, and website
- Start with small orders ($50–$100)
- Pay invoices early to boost your Paydex score

Important Note: Many vendors want to see that your business appears legitimate. If you're denied credit, it's often due to fundability issues—not creditworthiness. Double-check your online presence, business phone, and address consistency.

Step 3: Move to Tier 2 Credit Accounts

Once you have 3–5 positive tradelines reporting for 30–60 days, you can move up to Tier 2 credit accounts. These include more well-known brands and retail business cards that report to bureaus and may offer higher limits.

Tier 2 Accounts to Target:

- **Amazon Business Net-55** – Reports to D&B
- **Staples Business Credit** – Reports to D&B and Equifax
- **Home Depot Commercial Account** – Reports to Experian
- **Office Depot Business Credit** – Reports to D&B

These accounts typically don't require a personal guarantee if your business has tradelines and a strong Paydex score.

Action Step:

- Apply with your EIN
- Be prepared to show proof of revenue (bank statements or invoices)
- Avoid high balances—keep utilization under 30%

Step 4: Graduate to Tier 3 – Revolving Business Credit

After 60–90 days of responsible use, and at least 5–7 tradelines reporting, you can apply for **unsecured revolving credit**—including business credit cards and high-limit lines of credit.

Recommended Business Credit Cards:

- **Chase Ink Business Unlimited** – No annual fee, 0% APR intro

- **Amex Blue Business Plus** – 2x points, 0% APR intro
- **Capital One Spark Business** – Reports to all 3 bureaus

Credit lines and banks to consider:

- **Divvy** – Corporate expense card with credit-building reporting
- **Brex** – Offers high-limit cards with no personal guarantee
- **Fundbox or BlueVine** – Short-term working capital lines

Pro Tip: Some cards report to personal and business bureaus—so read the terms carefully. Focus on cards that report only to commercial bureaus to protect your personal credit.

Step 5: Monitor and Maintain Your Credit Profile

Once you've established credit, it's crucial to monitor and maintain it—just like you would with personal credit.

Here's how:

- Use Nav.com or CreditSignal (by D&B) for score alerts
- Pay all Net-30 and revolving accounts 5–10 days early
- Keep utilization low—under 30% if possible

- Add new accounts every 3–6 months to build depth
- Keep old accounts open to build history

What lenders look for:

- 5+ active tradelines
- Paydex score of 80+
- Low utilization
- At least 6 months of business banking activity
- Consistent EIN and business profile across all platforms

If your business meets these criteria, you'll qualify for higher credit limits, longer terms, and lender trust—opening the door to using this credit for real estate investments.

Common Pitfalls and How to Avoid Them

1. **Applying too soon:** Don't apply for Tier 2 or 3 credit before tradelines are reporting.
2. **Inconsistent business info:** Mismatched addresses, emails, or phone numbers will trigger red flags.
3. **Using personal credit by accident:** Make sure every application is EIN-based and doesn't require a PG (unless absolutely necessary).
4. **Late payments:** One late payment can drop your Paydex score dramatically.

5. **Vendor accounts that don't report:** Not all Net-30 vendors report—always confirm before applying.

Summary Action Plan

Week 1–2:

- Apply to 3–5 Tier 1 Net-30 vendors
- Order small and pay early
- Track payment due dates and receipts

Week 3–4:

- Register for a credit monitoring account on Nav.com
- Apply for your D-U-N-S number if you haven't already

Week 5–8:

- Begin applying for Tier 2 accounts
- Continue paying Tier 1 accounts early

Week 9–12:

- Apply for 1–2 business credit cards (Tier 3)
- Track your Paydex, Intelliscore, and Equifax scores monthly
- Keep all accounts active and utilization low

What's Next?

Now that you know how to build your business credit profile from scratch, you're ready to **access real capital**.

In the next chapter, we'll dive deep into accessing **high-limit business credit cards and lines of credit**—the kind of funding you can use to put down payments on properties, fund rehab work, or close deals that would otherwise require your own savings.

You've built the foundation and the profile—now let's start using it.

The Tradeline Blueprint

Three months had passed since Maya turned her hustle into a legitimate business. Keystone Acquisitions LLC now had a bank account, a business phone, a website, and even a small office suite downtown that she used for meetings and lender mail. But as she stared at her desk that Monday morning, something was still missing.

She needed funding—not promises, not spreadsheets, not another seminar—real capital. And she didn't want to use her personal credit ever again. Her eyes landed on a sticky note she had written in big, bold Sharpie weeks earlier: **"Business credit is the bridge."**

It was time to start building the bridge.

First Tradelines: Playing the Long Game

She started with the simplest, safest step: vendor credit. She remembered from her research that Net-30 accounts were the entry point. Maya pulled up Uline.com and created a business account using her EIN. She ordered $87 worth of shipping materials—bubble wrap, labels, and boxes—items she didn't even need yet, but knew she could store for later deals.

She wasn't sure they would approve her right away, but when the email came back that her order had shipped—and she had 30 days to pay—her heart jumped. It was working.

She did the same with Quill.com and Grainger. Each application took less than 10 minutes. Each used only her business information. Each reported to a credit bureau. Within a few days, she had nearly $400 in vendor credit available—no personal credit check, no personal guarantee.

And she paid every invoice on Day 5.

"I'm not here to float bills," she reminded herself. "I'm here to build a score."

The Waiting Game and the First Score

After 30 days, she signed into Nav.com to check her progress. At first, the reports showed "No data found." Maya was nervous. Had she done something wrong?

A week later, she checked again.

Boom. Three tradelines were now reporting under her EIN. Her D&B file had been activated. Her Paydex score was 80.

She felt like she had cracked a secret code. This was real. This was working.

She even got an email from Nav saying her profile was strong enough to qualify for her first true business credit card.

But Maya wasn't ready to jump too far ahead. She knew there were tiers to this.

Moving to Tier 2: The Retail Jump

At the 60-day mark, Maya had four solid tradelines. She decided to apply for the **Amazon Business Net-55** account. She filled out the form using only her EIN and business bank account. This time, the process felt smoother. Her business had history. It had payment behavior. It had proof.

She was approved instantly.

Next, she tried Staples. This one asked for additional documents, so she uploaded her Articles of Organization and bank statement. Two days later, the approval came through: $1,000 business credit line. Terms: Net-30.

Maya laughed. Just a few months ago, she couldn't get $300 from a lender without a hard pull. Now she was building a credit ecosystem—one that belonged to her business, not her name.

The confidence shift was massive.

She started thinking about how each of these accounts could be used for her next flip or rental. Boxes and office supplies from Uline. Paint and tools from Home Depot. Appliances from Amazon.

She wasn't spending just to spend. She was building access to cash flow tools. She was building credibility.

Tier 3: The Business Credit Card Play

After 90 days, Maya had seven tradelines reporting, an 82 Paydex score, and over $2,000 in vendor credit. She was ready for her first revolving business credit card.

She walked into her bank—Chase—and asked to apply for the **Ink Business Unlimited** card.

The banker pulled up her file and smiled. "Looks like your business has been active for a few months. Good deposits. Clean history. Let's see what we can do."

Maya waited in silence as the banker clicked through the screens. A minute later, he turned the monitor around and said, "You've been approved. $5,000 limit."

She didn't jump up and scream—but inside, she felt like she was flying.

This was the first time she'd been approved for a credit line that wasn't tied to her name or her personal FICO score. No personal guarantee. No personal liability. Just her business and its growing reputation.

She used the card to pay for staging furniture for an upcoming listing. The rewards alone covered her Nav subscription for the next six months.

The First Real Proof

The final confirmation came in the form of an unexpected email from a DSCR lender she'd spoken to months earlier. "Hey Maya, just circling back—do you have updated business credit data or any credit lines open?"

This time, she didn't hesitate.

She sent over her D&B report, her business credit card summary, and screenshots from her vendor accounts. Within 48 hours, the lender pre-approved her for a $150,000 line of credit—secured by a future property, backed by her business income.

She hadn't bought the property yet, but she had built something just as valuable: a real, fundable, scalable business credit profile.

Maya's journey is proof that anyone—from a solo wholesaler to a future property mogul—can create a credit infrastructure that fuels growth.

All it takes is a plan, consistency, and the willingness to play the long game.

In the next chapter, Maya—and you—will learn how to turn those credit profiles into **high-limit cards and powerful lines of credit** that can fund down payments, repairs, and even full real estate purchases.

The funding you want is already available. You just need to qualify the right way—and now you know how.

Chapter 4: Accessing High-Limit Business Credit Cards & Lines of Credit

At this point, you've set up your business the right way, created a fundable profile, and built a solid foundation of reporting trade lines. Now it's time to **move into the funding stage**—specifically, unlocking **high-limit business credit cards** and **lines of credit** that can be used to acquire, renovate, or scale your real estate investments.

This chapter will walk you through:

1. Understanding the power and flexibility of business credit cards
2. How to qualify for high-limit cards and lines of credit
3. How to apply for and use these credit tools properly
4. Smart strategies to avoid high interest and misuse
5. Tips for turning business credit into property funding

Step 1: Why Business Credit Cards and Lines Are Better for Investors

Unlike personal credit cards, **business credit cards:**

- Typically offer higher limits
- Don't affect your personal credit utilization

- Can be used solely for business purposes (tax deductible)
- Offer intro 0% APR offers for 6–18 months
- Are available even for newer businesses with established tradelines

Lines of credit (LOCs), whether revolving or term-based, provide cash you can draw from at any time, pay back, and reuse—ideal for down payments, repairs, or bridge funding between purchases and refinance events.

The key benefit? **These tools give you liquidity without using your own savings.** Used wisely, they become leverage machines for real estate acquisition and cash flow.

Step 2: Qualifying for High-Limit Business Credit Cards

Lenders and banks look at several key factors before issuing high-limit business credit. Here's what they want to see:

Minimum Requirements:

- At least **3–6 months in business**
- 5+ positive tradelines (vendor or retail accounts)
- Consistent revenue through a business bank account
- Strong Paydex or Intelliscore (80+ preferred)

- No red flags on business or personal credit (some lenders may soft pull personal credit to verify)

Bonus Factors:

- Having a relationship with the issuing bank
- Showing monthly cash flow of $3,000–$10,000+
- A business website, matching domain email, and online listings

Pro Tip: Even if a personal guarantee is required, these cards won't report to your personal credit as long as you pay on time—preserving your personal utilization.

Step 3: Best Business Credit Cards for Real Estate Investors

Below are some of the most popular and powerful business credit cards for investors:

1. Chase Ink Business Unlimited

- 0% APR for 12 months
- $750 sign-up bonus
- No annual fee
- Reports to business credit bureaus
- Great for: general spending, repairs, supplies

2. American Express Blue Business Plus

- 0% APR for 12 months
- 2x points on all purchases
- Soft pull application
- Flexible limits that scale with business growth
- Great for: large purchases, recurring costs

3. Capital One Spark 2% Cash Plus

- Unlimited 2% cash back
- May report to personal credit if not managed properly
- Great for: heavy spenders and high-volume operations

4. Divvy Business Card

- Expense tracking + built-in credit reporting
- No personal guarantee
- Works best for structured, recurring spend

Action Step:

- Apply for 1–2 of these cards after 90 days of building tradelines
- Use your EIN, not your SSN
- Start with smaller purchases and pay off before interest accrues

Step 4: Accessing Business Lines of Credit (LOCs)

Business lines of credit are more flexible than term loans or credit cards. They provide a **revolving cash limit**—often between $10,000 and $250,000—that you can use when needed.

Types of LOCs:

- **Traditional LOCs:** Issued by banks like Chase, Wells Fargo, or regional credit unions
- **Fintech LOCs:** Providers like BlueVine, Fundbox, and OnDeck offer faster approvals
- **Credit Union LOCs:** Local banks often offer better terms with lower interest

Requirements:

- 6+ months in business
- $5,000–$10,000+ in monthly revenue
- Business bank account
- Strong credit profile (some will check personal score)

Use Cases for Real Estate:

- Down payments on DSCR loans
- Covering renovation costs
- Short-term holding costs between financing events

- Appraisal fees, inspections, earnest money deposits

Pro Tip: Use lines of credit for cash flow timing—not long-term holding. The faster you repay, the more you can reuse.

Step 5: Avoiding Common Pitfalls

With great credit comes great responsibility. Misusing these tools can damage your business credit or create long-term debt problems.

Avoid These Mistakes:

- **Only making minimum payments:** Interest can balloon fast if you don't pay off in full before the 0% APR ends.
- **Using personal guarantees unnecessarily:** Some cards require it, but many don't—so check terms first.
- **Using business credit for personal expenses:** This can void protection and damage your business identity.
- **Not monitoring your utilization:** Even though cards don't show up on personal credit, utilization still impacts your business credit score.

Smart Practices:

- Pay early and often

- Use cards only for income-generating activities
- Track expenses clearly for tax deductions
- Limit open cards to what you can manage responsibly

Step 6: Turning Credit into Real Estate Capital

Once you've been approved for high-limit cards and credit lines, the question becomes: **How do you turn it into property?**

Real-World Scenarios:

- **$15,000 from a business credit card** covers a down payment on a $100,000 DSCR-financed property
- **$50,000 line of credit** funds a duplex rehab while you wait for refinance or flip sale
- **Multiple cards** (credit stacking) fund multiple acquisitions or fund one deal with diversified risk

Example Strategy:

1. Use $10,000 from Amex for down payment
2. Use $5,000 from Ink for inspection, title, and legal
3. Use LOC to cover 3 months of holding costs
4. Stabilize, refinance, and pay off credit with proceeds

By reinvesting profits and protecting credit utilization, you build a **repeatable funding engine**.

Summary Action Plan

1. Apply for 1–2 business credit cards with 0% intro APR
2. Open a business line of credit if revenue and tradelines allow
3. Only use funds for business-related, income-producing purposes
4. Repay early to maintain high credit scores
5. Track everything for tax and compliance purposes

Coming Up Next...

Now that you've unlocked access to high-limit cards and credit lines, the next step is to **use that funding to actually close on real estate**.

In the next chapter, we'll break down the entire **step-by-step process of funding and closing a real estate deal** using your business credit—from offer to keys.

Get ready. You're no longer just building credit—you're building an empire.

Credit is Capital

The sun hadn't even come up yet when Maya opened her laptop and logged into her business bank account. She was wired—not from caffeine, but from something deeper. The duplex she had her eye on was about to hit the market that morning, and she didn't want to lose it. But the question on her mind wasn't *can I afford it?*

It was *how do I fund it with business credit?*

For the first time in her life, Maya had options.

The Funding Game

Three months earlier, Maya had built her business credit profile with vendor accounts and a few retail tradelines. Today, she was ready to step into the big leagues.

She walked into her local Chase branch with her business checkbook in hand. The same banker who helped her open the account last quarter greeted her with a smile.

"How's Keystone Acquisitions doing?" he asked.

"Growing," Maya said. "I'd like to apply for a business credit card today."

The banker pulled up her file. "Looks like you're pre-qualified for the Chase Ink Business Unlimited. Want to go for that?"

She nodded. Ten minutes later, she walked out with a $7,000 approval—0% APR for 12 months.

It wasn't just the number that made her grin. It was the validation. Her business had earned this. No personal credit pulled. No co-signer. Just proof that she was playing the game right.

The Right Card at the Right Time

Back home, she reviewed her new credit dashboard. Her D&B Paydex score was 84. Experian Intelliscore? A respectable 78. More importantly, her limits were climbing.

In the last 30 days, she'd been approved for:

- The **Chase Ink card** for $7,000
- An **American Express Blue Business Plus** for $10,000
- A **Divvy expense account** that gave her weekly spending power of $2,500

All in her business's name. All built from scratch within six months.

She smiled as she remembered how it all started—with a few boxes from Uline and a pack of toner from Quill. Small moves. Big payoff.

Now it was time to level up again.

The Line of Credit Call

That afternoon, Maya jumped on a call with a lending advisor from BlueVine. They offered business lines of credit up to $250,000 based on banking activity and credit history.

The woman on the line, Amanda, sounded impressed. "Your business banking history is clean. Your revenue is steady. And your credit profile checks out. We can offer you a revolving line of $40,000 to start."

Maya paused. That was more than enough to make her duplex offer competitive.

Amanda continued, "You can draw as needed. Interest only applies to what you use. No early payoff penalties."

That night, Maya signed the offer letter digitally. She now had the power to move quickly on deals—and she didn't have to dip into her personal savings to do it.

She had become the bank.

Making the Offer

With her Chase Ink and BlueVine LOC active, Maya contacted her realtor and sent over the offer package: a full-price offer with a 15-day close, $10,000 earnest money deposit, and proof of funds from her business LOC.

Most investors would take 30–45 days. Maya was ready in 15.

The seller, a retired landlord with too many properties and not enough patience, accepted the offer that same night.

Maya had just secured her second property—without ever touching her personal bank account.

Credit in Action

The next week was a flurry of activity. She used:

- $7,200 from Amex to pay the inspection company, appraisal fee, and light plumbing repairs
- $5,000 from her BlueVine LOC for closing costs and earnest money
- $4,000 from Chase Ink for staging, listing photography, and utility deposits

Each card was paid down the moment rent checks hit her business account. And because they were all 0% APR for the first 12 months, she wasn't paying interest—just using leverage.

Her cash stayed in the bank. Her equity grew with every payment. Her business credit profile got even stronger with each transaction.

She wasn't worried about the balances because she had a plan—and predictable rental income.

Reflection: From Scrappy to Strategic

Sitting at her dining table a week later, Maya opened a spreadsheet. It wasn't full of dreams—it was full of reality:

- Two active properties
- Over $20,000 in usable business credit
- A $40,000 LOC
- Monthly cash flow of $1,700 after expenses
- A credit score on the rise

More importantly, she was in control.

What had once seemed impossible—buying property without savings or W-2 income—was now her business model.

She had built it, brick by brick, line by line.

Maya leaned back and smiled. She wasn't just buying properties anymore. She was building a business that funded itself.

The duplex would cash-flow in 30 days. The credit cards would be paid down in 60. And she already had her eye on a triplex across town.

Credit wasn't a crutch. It was a catapult.

Chapter 5: Business Loans & DSCR Mortgages

Now that you've accessed high-limit business credit cards and lines of credit, it's time to explore **longer-term funding options**—specifically, **business loans** and **DSCR (Debt Service Coverage Ratio) mortgages**. These tools allow you to finance entire properties without relying on personal tax returns or income documentation.

This chapter will guide you through:

1. Understanding business loans vs. DSCR mortgages
2. Preparing your business for loan underwriting
3. How DSCR mortgages work and when to use them
4. Choosing the right lenders
5. A step-by-step walkthrough of applying for each type

Step 1: Understanding Business Loans vs. DSCR Mortgages

These two types of financing serve different purposes in your real estate investing journey:

Business Loans:

- Offered based on your business income and credit profile

- Used for general business purposes, including real estate, renovations, and working capital
- Typically short to mid-term (1–5 years)
- Available from banks, credit unions, and online lenders
- May be unsecured or secured with assets

DSCR Mortgages:

- Designed specifically for real estate investors
- Based on the property's income—not your personal income or credit
- No tax returns or pay stubs required
- Loans range from 15–30 years
- Great for buy-and-hold rental properties

Both types can work together: for example, using a business LOC to fund a down payment, and a DSCR loan to fund the purchase.

Step 2: Preparing Your Business for a Loan

Before applying for either type of loan, your business should meet these criteria:

Basic Requirements:

- Business entity in good standing (LLC or Corp)

- EIN and business checking account
- 6+ months of revenue (for most fintech lenders; banks may require 1+ year)
- Strong business credit profile (Paydex 80+, low credit utilization)
- Clean online presence (website, domain email, Google listing)

Documents You May Need:

- Business bank statements (last 3–6 months)
- Articles of Incorporation/Organization
- Business license (if required by your state/county)
- Proof of business address (utility bill or lease)
- D-U-N-S number and credit report access

Pro Tip: Even if your business is new, strong vendor history and good banking activity can get you approved.

Step 3: Understanding DSCR Mortgages

A **DSCR loan** is a real estate investor's best friend. It allows you to borrow based on the **property's ability to pay for itself**, rather than your W-2 income or tax returns.

How It Works:

- DSCR is calculated by dividing the property's monthly income by its monthly mortgage payment.
- Example: A property rents for $2,000/month and the mortgage is $1,600/month = DSCR of 1.25.
- Most lenders want a DSCR of at least 1.0–1.25 to approve the loan.

Key Features:

- No personal income required
- Can close under your LLC
- 20–30% down payment typically required
- Available for single-family, duplex, triplex, and fourplex properties
- Loan terms of 30 years with interest-only options

Lenders will look at:

- Property rent estimates (based on appraiser or market rents)
- Your business credit profile
- Recent property taxes, insurance estimates, and HOA dues (if applicable)

Step 4: Finding the Right Lenders

Business Loans:

- **Traditional Banks:** Chase, Bank of America, Wells Fargo (slower, but lower rates)
- **Online Lenders:** BlueVine, Fundbox, OnDeck, Kabbage (fast approvals, higher rates)
- **Credit Unions:** Often offer lower fees and better customer service
- **SBA Loans:** 7(a) and 504 programs offer long-term financing, but have stricter requirements

DSCR Mortgage Lenders:

- **Specialized DSCR Lenders:** Kiavi, Visio, Lima One, CoreVest, Velocity Mortgage
- **Mortgage Brokers:** Can connect you with multiple DSCR lenders
- **Hard Money Lenders:** Can offer DSCR-style loans at higher rates, but faster closings

Pro Tip: Avoid lenders who try to pull your personal credit or require tax returns unless you're seeking a conventional loan.

Step 5: How to Apply — Step-by-Step

For a Business Loan or Line of Credit:

1. **Gather Documents:** EIN, Articles of Incorporation, last 3–6 months of business bank statements, business license
2. **Apply Online or In-Person:** Start with the bank you already use
3. **Wait for Underwriting:** May take 1–5 business days
4. **Get Funding:** If approved, funds may be available same-day for fintech lenders or within 1–2 weeks for banks

For a DSCR Loan:

1. **Find a Property:** Property must be income-producing or tenant-ready
2. **Submit Loan Application:** Include property address, rent estimate, and business info
3. **Provide Supporting Documents:** LLC docs, EIN, business bank statements, and property details
4. **Appraisal & Underwriting:** Property is appraised to determine rental value
5. **Close the Deal:** Funds are used for purchase; title and escrow handled by lender

Estimated Timeline:

- Business loan: 1–2 weeks

- DSCR loan: 2–4 weeks (can be faster with the right team)

Common Mistakes to Avoid

1. **Applying too soon:** Build business credit first and ensure revenue is consistent
2. **Mixing personal and business income:** This can disqualify you or cause tax problems
3. **Using personal guarantee unnecessarily:** Some lenders may sneak it in—read the fine print
4. **Choosing the wrong property for DSCR:** If rent is too low, the DSCR won't qualify
5. **Not negotiating rates or terms:** Many lenders will match or beat competing offers if asked

Summary Action Plan

Week 1:

- Evaluate your business credit and revenue history
- Choose which path to pursue first: business loan or DSCR mortgage

Week 2:

- Research lenders and gather necessary documents

- Apply to one business lender and one DSCR lender (if you have a property identified)

Week 3–4:

- Complete underwriting process
- Use approved funding to make offers, pay for inspections, or close deals

What's Next?

You now understand how to secure long-term capital for your real estate business—without touching your personal credit. In the next chapter, we'll walk through a **real deal scenario**: using business credit to fund a real estate purchase from offer to close.

You'll learn how to:

- Combine cards, LOCs, and DSCR funding
- Handle escrow, inspections, and rehab costs
- Protect your credit while scaling your portfolio

Let's put your knowledge into practice—and get the keys to your next property.

The Power of the Property That Pays for Itself

Maya stood across the street from a tan duplex with blue shutters in a quiet Orlando neighborhood. It wasn't glamorous, but it was solid—two units, long-term tenants, low maintenance. Her agent had called the night before and said, "This is the one. You can get it below market, and the numbers work."

She already knew the math: $1,900 rent per side, $3,800 total per month. Property taxes were low. The seller wanted $310,000. Maya checked her phone again—this one had potential.

But this time, she wasn't looking to patch funding together with credit cards or lines of credit. She wanted a 30-year play. A deal she could hold, cash flow, and scale off of. She wanted a **DSCR mortgage**.

The DSCR Discovery

Just three months earlier, Maya hadn't even heard the term "DSCR." Then she found an article explaining that investors could finance properties based on the **income the property generated—not their personal W-2 income**.

It clicked immediately. She didn't have years of tax returns showing a huge salary. But she had a business. She had credit. And she had properties that paid for themselves.

She looked back at her laptop notes:

> "DSCR = Rental Income / PITI (Principal, Interest, Taxes, Insurance)."

As long as that number was over 1.0, she could qualify. The higher, the better.

The duplex she just toured would rent for $3,800. With a 25% down payment and a DSCR mortgage, the projected mortgage was just under $2,600—including taxes and insurance. That gave her a DSCR of **1.46**. Solid.

The Business Loan Warm-Up

Before diving into DSCR, Maya wanted a financial cushion. She logged into her business bank account and uploaded her last 6 months of revenue to BlueVine.

Three days later, she was approved for a $50,000 **business line of credit**.

"Use what you need, when you need it," the approval email said.

That same afternoon, she applied with OnDeck and secured a **$30,000 working capital loan**, fixed at 12 months. The payments were high, but she didn't mind. It was bridge money—flexible, fast, and in her business name only.

These weren't investments. They were leverage. A way to move with speed while her DSCR lender processed the bigger loan.

Getting the DSCR Loan

Maya contacted a broker she found through a real estate investor podcast. His name was Leon, and he specialized in DSCR deals.

She emailed him everything:

- Property address
- LLC docs
- Rent comps
- Articles of Organization
- Business bank statements
- A screenshot of her business credit report

Within hours, he replied: "This will fly. You've got a great DSCR, and the area is landlord-friendly. I'll run it through underwriting."

The next week was a whirlwind. Appraisal. Title search. Rent estimates. Maya paid for it all using her business Amex. Every expense logged under Keystone Acquisitions. Clean. Professional. Separated from her personal life.

The appraisal came back at $325,000. Even better than expected.

Her down payment? $77,500. She pulled $30,000 from the

OnDeck loan and the rest from her LOC and cash flow reserves.

The Close

Closing day was quiet. Maya sat across from the title agent, signed the documents, and smiled when she saw the lender's name: Velocity Mortgage, LLC—funded through a 30-year DSCR note with a 7.25% fixed interest rate.

No personal credit pulled. No tax returns. No employment verification. Just her business and the income the property produced.

The duplex was hers.

The tenants stayed. The cash flowed. Maya had done it again.

Scaling the Strategy

After the deal closed, Maya reflected on what had changed.

Just 10 months ago, she was stuck—running everything through her personal name, limited by banks that didn't understand her business.

Now, she had:

- Over $100,000 in business credit
- $80,000 in business loans and LOCs
- Two rental properties—one fully DSCR financed

- A cash-flowing business that was building real estate equity

The real secret? **She had become lendable—on the terms that worked for her.**

A New Kind of Leverage

That night, Maya opened her laptop and reviewed her next steps:

- Reinvest rental profits into paying down her LOC
- Apply for another DSCR mortgage next quarter
- Use her BlueVine LOC to fund the down payment on the next deal

She didn't feel stretched. She felt empowered.

Her goal wasn't to own 100 properties. Her goal was to own 10 free and clear—each one funded creatively, safely, and profitably through her business.

She turned off her laptop and poured a glass of wine. The duplex she'd just bought was already paying its own mortgage.

That was the magic of business credit and DSCR.

Not just getting funded—but **getting free**.

Chapter 6: Funding a Real Estate Purchase Step-by-Step

You've built your business credit, secured high-limit cards and credit lines, and explored loan options like DSCR mortgages. Now it's time to pull everything together and walk through the complete process of **funding a real estate deal using business credit**.

This chapter will guide you step-by-step through:

1. Sourcing the property
2. Structuring the funding
3. Managing the transaction from offer to close
4. Using business credit cards and LOCs for key costs
5. Keeping the purchase separate from your personal finances

Step 1: Sourcing a Deal That Qualifies

The first step is finding a **cash-flowing property** that meets the requirements of business-friendly lenders and DSCR loan programs.

What to look for:

- Single-family, duplex, triplex, or fourplex

- Long-term or short-term rental potential
- Low maintenance and minor repairs
- Strong local rental demand
- Price range that aligns with your available credit and funding options

DSCR Requirement: The property's gross monthly rent must be **equal to or greater** than the monthly mortgage payment (PITI). Aim for a **DSCR of 1.2+** for easier approval.

Pro Tip: Use rent estimation tools like Rentometer or Zillow Rental Manager to calculate local market rents. Then estimate your monthly mortgage using online DSCR calculators.

Step 2: Structuring Your Funding Strategy

Once you've identified a property, build your **funding stack**—a combination of business credit cards, business loans, LOCs, and mortgage financing.

Typical funding stack might include:

- **Business Credit Cards:** Used for inspections, appraisals, title fees, and contractor deposits
- **Business LOC:** Used for earnest money, down payment, or holding costs
- **DSCR Mortgage:** Used to fund 70–80% of the

purchase price

Example:

- Purchase price: $250,000
- DSCR loan: $175,000 (70%)
- Down payment: $75,000
- Use $50,000 from business LOC, $10,000 from a working capital loan, and $15,000 from reserves

Pro Tip: Create a spreadsheet or project budget before making an offer so you know exactly where funds are coming from and how repayment will be managed.

Step 3: Making the Offer and Showing Proof of Funds

With your funding plan in place, make a competitive offer. If working with a DSCR lender, they may provide you with a **pre-approval letter**.

What you'll need to include with your offer:

- Pre-approval letter (DSCR lender or business loan provider)
- Proof of funds (screenshot or letter showing credit line availability)
- Earnest money deposit (typically 1–3% of purchase price)

Tip for using business credit: Transfer earnest money from your business LOC to your business bank account and write the check directly from the business. This keeps all expenses separate and shows professionalism to real estate agents and sellers.

Step 4: Managing the Transaction (Inspections, Appraisals, Title)

Once your offer is accepted, the transaction process begins. Here's how to use business credit strategically at each step:

1. Inspection Fees

- Pay using a business credit card for tax deductibility and easy tracking
- Cost: $300–$600 (depending on property type)

2. Appraisal

- DSCR lenders require an appraisal (cost: $450–$800)
- Use business credit card or line of credit to pay and ensure it's expensed to the LLC

3. Title, Insurance, & Closing Costs

- Work with a title company that can invoice your business
- Request a settlement statement early to plan your credit usage

- Use LOC or business card for closing costs not covered by loan

Tip: Ask your DSCR lender if you can roll some closing costs into the loan (many allow this).

Step 5: Closing the Deal Through Your Business

At closing, the property title should be transferred directly to your LLC or Corporation—not your personal name. This reinforces the business structure and ensures full asset separation.

Closing checklist:

- Title transferred to LLC
- Business name and EIN on all closing documents
- Funds wired from business bank account
- Mortgage closed under the LLC (for DSCR)

Important: Ensure all payments made during the deal—from inspections to earnest money—are made using your business credit sources and tracked via your accounting software or business expense tracker.

Step 6: Post-Close Management Using Business Credit

After closing, your business credit can continue working for you:

Use business credit for:

- Minor renovations and repairs
- Furniture, appliances, and landscaping
- Marketing and tenant screening services
- Property management software and automation tools

Set up automatic payments on your business cards and loans to build stronger credit and avoid interest.

Cash Flow Tip: Use rental income to pay off business credit lines as fast as possible, freeing up credit for the next deal.

Common Mistakes to Avoid

1. **Paying for expenses personally** – Co-mingling funds can ruin liability protection
2. **Overleveraging one source** – Diversify between cards, loans, and LOCs to manage risk
3. **Using credit without a cash flow plan** – Don't borrow if the deal won't cover the repayments
4. **Skipping inspections or appraisals** – Business-backed loans still require due diligence
5. **Failing to close in the business name** – This prevents you from using DSCR and asset protection benefits

Action Plan

Pre-Offer:

- Find a property with DSCR of 1.2+
- Build a funding stack using business credit sources
- Get DSCR pre-approval letter and proof of funds

Offer to Close:

- Submit offer with supporting docs
- Pay for inspection and appraisal using business cards
- Manage title and escrow using business LOC or cash
- Close in LLC name with DSCR loan

Post-Close:

- Use business credit to furnish, market, or renovate
- Set repayment strategy using rental income
- Monitor credit utilization and prepare for your next deal

Coming Up Next...

You've just completed a full real estate transaction using business credit and DSCR financing. In the next chapter, we'll talk about **scaling with multiple properties**, how to manage your growing credit stack, and how to get approved for higher limits as your portfolio grows.

Let's keep building.

The Deal That Paid Her Back

Maya stood outside the title company's office with a manila folder tucked under her arm and her laptop bag slung over her shoulder. She checked her phone one last time. Everything was ready—the funds had been wired from her business account, the DSCR lender had cleared the file, and the closing statement had her LLC's name at the top.

This wasn't her first deal—but it was the first she had funded entirely through business credit.

No personal money. No credit pulled. No explaining herself to bankers.

It had taken months of setup, but this moment—this building on the corner with two tenants paying rent—was the payoff.

Finding the Right Property

Two weeks earlier, Maya's agent sent her a pocket listing—a compact fourplex on the edge of a fast-growing college town. Three units were rented. The fourth just needed paint and a new appliance package. Asking price: $415,000. Monthly gross rent potential: $5,000. With some quick math, Maya realized the DSCR would be close to 1.35. Perfect.

But more important than the numbers was this: Maya had everything lined up.

She had already mapped her funding stack.

- $55,000 from her business LOC
- $12,000 on her Chase Ink business card
- $8,000 available on Amex
- DSCR pre-approval from CoreVest for up to 75% LTV

She wasn't just hoping the deal would work. She *knew* it could.

Making the Offer with Business Power

She emailed her agent the offer documents—LLC name, pre-approval letter, and proof of funds. Her earnest money, $5,000, came straight from her BlueVine line of credit into her business checking account. The check was printed under Keystone Acquisitions, LLC.

When the seller's agent called and said, "We have higher offers, but your buyer looks serious," Maya smiled. That's what good preparation does—it builds trust. Her offer was accepted in less than 24 hours.

Managing the Process Like a Business

The next 10 days were packed.

She scheduled the inspection and paid the $525 fee using her Amex Blue Business Plus. The inspector emailed the report to her business domain address, and Maya forwarded it directly to her DSCR lender.

Next came the appraisal, which cost $700 and was invoiced directly to her business. She paid early.

The appraised value came back at $435,000. That meant more equity than expected—and gave her extra negotiating power on the title side.

When the title company asked how she'd be handling closing costs, Maya pulled up her spreadsheet. She had $14,500 allocated from her LOC for closing, and $7,000 budgeted for repairs from her business card.

Everything was documented. Every dollar accounted for.

She didn't just feel like an investor—she felt like a CFO.

Closing in Control

On closing day, she double-checked the closing disclosure. The buyer was listed as "Keystone Acquisitions, LLC." The DSCR lender was CoreVest. The down payment had been wired from her BlueVine LOC. The repairs would be covered on her Ink card.

The tenants didn't even know a change had occurred. Rent would now be paid to a new property manager—contracted through Maya's LLC, paid via her business account, and tracked in her property management software.

She had gone from finding the deal to closing without once dipping into her personal funds or tying her name to the mortgage.

This wasn't just a real estate purchase—it was a credit-funded business acquisition.

After the Close

That weekend, Maya visited the vacant unit. She walked through with a contractor and showed him the list: paint, cabinet touch-up, new fridge and stove. $3,500 all-in.

She handed him a deposit via a business credit card, already labeled in her accounting app.

Two weeks later, a new tenant signed a lease.

The entire property was now cash flowing. The monthly mortgage was $3,150. Gross rent was $5,000. After expenses, she netted $1,200 per month—on a property she didn't personally fund.

And best of all?

She still had over $40,000 in credit availability to use for her next deal.

Reflecting on the Shift

Maya sat at her desk that night and opened her whiteboard app. She wrote in bold:

> "1 Deal Funded Entirely With Business Credit = Infinite Possibility."

She had learned how to use credit not just as a tool—but as a **system**. Business cards for inspections and appraisals. LOC for deposits and closing. DSCR for the big financing. Rental income to pay it all back.

It wasn't magic. It was method.

And she could do it again.

Chapter 7: Scaling with Multiple Properties

You've closed your first deal using business credit. Now the real question becomes: **how do you scale**?

The goal isn't just to use business credit once—it's to build a **repeatable, scalable system** that allows you to acquire multiple properties with minimal personal risk and increasing leverage. In this chapter, we'll cover exactly how to do that.

What You'll Learn in This Chapter:

1. How to build a scalable credit and lending system
2. How to increase your credit limits and access new funding
3. Managing multiple properties with credit protection
4. When and how to refinance or recycle credit
5. Tracking, automation, and reporting for ongoing scaling

Step 1: Build a Replicable Funding Blueprint

Every property you purchase should follow a consistent, proven system. Here's a sample framework that you can copy and adjust:

Your Scalable Property Funding Model:

- **Business Credit Cards** for initial costs (inspection, appraisal, earnest money)
- **Business LOCs or Term Loans** for down payments and closing costs
- **DSCR Mortgages** for 70–80% of the purchase price
- **Rental Income** to repay credit lines and cards
- **Property #1's profits** fund **Property #2's down payment**

By standardizing how you fund each deal, you reduce mental stress and increase your speed. Each property becomes a *project*, funded by tools your business already controls.

Step 2: Increase Credit Limits and Access More Capital

After 3–6 months of on-time payments and solid usage, most lenders will review your profile and offer limit increases. Here's how to approach this strategically:

Business Credit Cards:

- Call issuers and request soft-pull limit increases
- Show strong revenue and payment history
- Keep utilization below 30% for optimal increases

Lines of Credit:

- Ask for a credit limit review every 6–12 months

- Submit updated bank statements and rent roll
- Consider opening additional LOCs with new lenders (while keeping utilization low on existing accounts)

New Lenders to Explore:

- American Express (Business Gold/Plum)
- Truist and PNC for business LOCs
- Lendio, Credibly, and Fundbox for term loans

Pro Tip: Always keep one or two business credit lines completely unused—this gives you instant access to emergency funds and strengthens your DSCR loan applications.

Step 3: Managing Multiple Properties Without Financial Chaos

Once you own more than one property, systems and organization become your secret weapon.

Create the Following Systems:

- A **dedicated business checking account per property** (or at least per entity)
- **Monthly financial dashboard** tracking: income, expenses, debt usage, rent collection, and credit utilization
- **Automated expense tracking** using tools like

QuickBooks, Xero, or Wave Accounting

- **A business email alias per property** to manage maintenance requests, tenant communication, and lender updates

Leverage Credit Safely:

- Never use 100% of your credit limits
- Avoid using short-term credit for long-term expenses (i.e., don't furnish rentals on a 12-month loan unless the ROI is immediate)
- Repay high-interest accounts first—even if balances are smaller

Step 4: Recycling Capital with Refinance & Cash-Out Strategies

Once you've stabilized a rental property and proven its income, you can **refinance the property and pay off your business credit**—freeing up your limits to repeat the process.

Types of Refinancing Options:

- **DSCR Refinance**: Based on rental income, no tax returns needed
- **Cash-Out Refinance**: Pull out equity to repay debt or fund next purchase

- **HELOCs on Business-Owned Properties** (available through certain lenders)

Timing Your Refinance:

- Wait 6–12 months after acquisition
- Show clean payment history and full occupancy
- Prepare updated rent rolls, business bank statements, and credit reports

Why This Works: You're essentially using the **BRRRR method** (Buy, Rehab, Rent, Refinance, Repeat), but powered by business credit instead of personal savings.

Step 5: Monitor, Automate, and Prepare to Scale Again

To keep growing, you must monitor both your properties and your credit profiles.

Weekly Tasks:

- Review credit card usage and payments
- Monitor new trade lines and reports via Nav or CreditSignal
- Check rent collection and expense ratios

Monthly Tasks:

- Update your profit and loss sheet per property

- Request credit limit increases from vendors or banks
- Reevaluate your current funding stack and liquidity buffer

Quarterly Tasks:

- Evaluate performance of each property
- Meet with your lender(s) to discuss pre-approvals for the next purchase
- Conduct a soft credit check on your business to ensure no negative marks

Tools to Use:

- **Nav.com** – for credit monitoring
- **QuickBooks or Wave** – for cash flow tracking
- **Stessa or Rentec Direct** – for property-specific accounting
- **Gusto or Bench** – for business financial reporting and payroll (if applicable)

Common Mistakes to Avoid While Scaling

1. **Over-leveraging credit without rental coverage**
2. **Ignoring credit utilization and score drops**
3. **Using personal funds out of habit or emotion**

4. **Closing credit accounts after paying them off** – this can hurt your business credit
5. **Buying properties too quickly without stabilizing previous ones**

Remember: speed is not the goal—**sustainability and predictability are**.

Summary Action Plan

Immediately:

- Standardize your property funding model
- Create a checklist for each new acquisition
- Request credit limit increases where eligible

Next 30 Days:

- Open a new business LOC or card if needed
- Systematize tracking of each property's cash flow and expenses
- Analyze at least one refinance opportunity

Next 60–90 Days:

- Refinance or pay down current credit
- Begin the acquisition process for your next deal
- Track results and repeat your proven system

Coming Up Next...

You now have the framework to scale your real estate business using business credit. In the next chapter, we'll go into **avoiding legal, financial, and credit-related mistakes** that can ruin your progress—and show you how to protect your business and personal assets while continuing to grow.

Let's keep building smart, sustainable wealth.

One Property at a Time, Forever

Maya's phone buzzed with a calendar reminder: "Property #3 rent due." She smiled—not because she needed the reminder, but because it was the third property she had acquired in under a year. And this time, she didn't feel overwhelmed.

She felt organized. She felt powerful.

Because Maya had figured out something most investors miss—**it wasn't about owning the most properties, it was about building the most sustainable system**.

The Turning Point

It started two months ago, right after the closing on her DSCR-financed fourplex. The success of that deal gave her momentum, but it also came with new responsibility—four units, eight tenants, and multiple payment due dates.

She realized if she wanted to keep going, she needed a **scaling plan**—something repeatable, organized, and efficient.

She opened her laptop and created a simple note titled: **"Maya's Repeatable Funding System"**

At the top, she listed her resources:

- Two business credit cards with $10,000+ limits
- A $50,000 business line of credit
- A DSCR lender who trusted her
- Two rental properties with full occupancy
- One strong business credit profile

The question became: *How do I use this same model again and again?*

A Repeatable Process

The first step was documenting every phase of her previous deal: sourcing, funding, closing, and management. She broke it down into stages and listed exactly which tools she used for what:

- **Chase Ink card** for inspections and appraisals
- **Amex Blue** for renovations and contractor deposits
- **BlueVine LOC** for down payments and closing costs

- **DSCR mortgage** for 75% LTV funding
- **Rental income** to repay credit lines within 90 days

It was like solving her own puzzle, and the pieces fit perfectly.

She turned it into a template. The next deal would follow this path—and so would every one after.

Growing Smarter, Not Faster

As new deals came in, Maya made a critical decision: she would not pursue multiple closings at once. Instead, she would use a **"one-in-one-out" model**.

She'd fund and stabilize one property, **then refinance or repay**, and only then would she begin the next acquisition.

This rhythm helped her avoid burnout. And it made her smarter. With each property, she learned what worked, what didn't, and how to improve.

Her second duplex? Funded in 30 days using a mix of a $15,000 business credit card draw and a DSCR loan. After 90 days of full occupancy, she refinanced, paid off the card, and restored her credit capacity.

Three months later, she was ready for deal number four.

Tools, Teams, and Automation

By the time she owned three properties, Maya knew she

needed to build systems. She signed up for **Stessa** to track rental income and expenses. She opened **QuickBooks Online** to link her business cards and automate bookkeeping.

Each property had its own nickname and bank account:

- "Lincoln" – her first single-family rental
- "Palms" – the fourplex with the best curb appeal
- "Willow" – her newest duplex with short-term rental potential

She even created a new business email alias for each property—willow@keystoneacquisitions.com—for maintenance requests and tenant communication.

Now, when a rent payment came in or a contractor needed to be paid, it was handled **by the system—not by Maya's memory**.

The Power of Credit Discipline

Maya was strict with her credit. She kept all utilization under 30%. She paid off balances twice a month. She rotated use across cards to keep them active and reporting.

Every quarter, she scheduled a 30-minute meeting with herself to request credit line increases, review property cash flow, and research new lenders.

Because of this discipline, her credit limits grew:

- Chase Ink: $10,000 → $18,000
- Amex Blue: $12,000 → $20,000
- BlueVine LOC: $50,000 → $75,000

She wasn't just growing a portfolio. She was growing her *credit ceiling*—the ability to fund bigger deals, faster, with less friction.

Scaling with Control

A year ago, Maya would've been anxious with three closings, thousands in monthly expenses, and multiple tenants calling. Now, she was at peace. Her business ran on structure. Her acquisitions ran on repeat.

She didn't rush. She didn't panic. She didn't overextend.

Each deal had a purpose. Each credit card swipe had a repayment plan.

By creating a process, Maya had done what most investors never do: **she had scaled without stress**.

The Vision Ahead

That night, she opened her notebook and wrote three goals:

1. Own 10 income-generating properties
2. Keep credit utilization below 20%

3. Have every property pay for the next one

Beneath it, she added a fourth:

> "Live off rental income. Let credit build the future."

Maya had started her journey with a single Uline account and a dream. Now, she owned three properties, had over $100,000 in available credit, and a growing list of pre-approved deals.

But more importantly, she had **a system that could scale forever**.

Chapter 8: Avoiding Common Mistakes and Legal Issues

As your business credit and real estate portfolio grow, so do the risks. While business credit offers power and flexibility, improper use or mismanagement can damage your credit profile, expose you to legal risk, or even jeopardize your business.

This chapter will walk you through:

1. The most common mistakes made by new investors using business credit
2. Legal risks you must avoid when using credit for real estate
3. Properly separating business and personal finances
4. Staying compliant with lenders, the IRS, and state regulations
5. Protecting your credit and reputation as you grow

Step 1: Recognize the Most Common Credit Mistakes

Let's start with the top business credit missteps that slow down—or ruin—growth:

1. Co-mingling business and personal funds

- Using personal cards for business expenses or vice versa

can lead to legal liability and accounting issues

- Tip: Always use a business credit card and checking account, even for small purchases

2. Applying for credit too soon or too often

- Applying before your business is ready (no tradelines, low revenue, inconsistent data) often leads to denials
- Too many applications in a short period can trigger red flags and soft-pull denials

3. Over-leveraging business credit

- Just because you're approved for $100K doesn't mean you should use it all
- Use only what is needed for income-producing activity (like acquiring or improving real estate)

4. Failing to pay on time or not tracking due dates

- One late payment can hurt your business credit score for months
- Tip: Set up autopay or schedule bi-weekly checks of your accounts

5. Closing business credit accounts

- Closing a card after paying it off can hurt your business credit age and limit profile

- Keep accounts open and active with small monthly charges

Step 2: Avoid Legal Pitfalls with Proper Structuring

Many new investors make the mistake of treating their LLC like a nameplate instead of a legal entity. If your business isn't properly structured, you risk **piercing the corporate veil**—which means creditors or courts can come after you personally.

Avoid These Legal Pitfalls:

- Failing to separate business and personal assets
- Signing business credit agreements with personal guarantees (when not needed)
- Using your home address for business purposes without protection
- Not renewing your LLC or corporate registration annually
- Paying contractors or vendors from personal accounts for property expenses

Pro Tip: Keep all documentation organized. Lenders, auditors, and legal counsel may request:

- LLC or corporate formation docs

- Articles of Incorporation
- Business bank statements
- Business lease (if using a virtual or physical office)
- Operating agreement (especially if you have partners)

Step 3: Separate Business and Personal Finances—For Real

Separation isn't just for safety—it's for growth. Lenders are more likely to approve you when your business looks *legitimate, profitable, and independent.*

Here's how to separate the right way:

- Use your **EIN** for all credit and banking applications
- Open and maintain a **business checking account** (never use a personal one)
- Pay all business expenses using your **business cards and LOCs**
- Receive all rental income into your business account
- Pay yourself with a salary or owner's draw (instead of random transfers)

Accounting Best Practices:

- Use **QuickBooks**, **Wave**, or **Bench** to categorize income and expenses

- Hire a CPA familiar with real estate and small business credit
- Maintain clear records for all income, credit use, and property costs

Step 4: Stay Compliant with Lenders, the IRS, and State Agencies

Business credit is not a loophole—it's a professional tool. To keep it working in your favor, make sure your business is compliant at all times.

IRS Requirements:

- File taxes annually using your EIN and business structure (Schedule C, 1120S, etc.)
- Report all income, including rent, loan proceeds, and interest earned
- Maintain receipts and proof of credit card expenses for deductions

State Requirements:

- Renew your LLC or corporate status annually with your state
- Keep your registered agent and address current
- File annual reports or pay business privilege taxes (in some states)

Lender Compliance:

- Understand your loan covenants (minimum DSCR, occupancy rate, insurance)
- Respond to documentation requests in a timely fashion
- Avoid misrepresentation (e.g., saying a property is fully leased when it's not)

Step 5: Protect Your Business Credit and Reputation

Your business credit profile is one of your most valuable assets. Guard it like your personal credit score—or even more carefully.

How to Protect Your Profile:

- Monitor reports monthly using **Nav**, **CreditSignal**, or **Equifax Business**
- Use no more than 30% of available credit across all accounts
- Request removal of inaccurate negative items with dispute letters
- Avoid hard inquiries by asking lenders for soft pull options or pre-approval
- Build relationships with your lenders—relationship banking leads to better terms and higher limits

Reputation Tip: When working with DSCR lenders, brokers, contractors, or partners—your responsiveness, professionalism, and organization all matter. Keep clean records, communicate clearly, and follow through.

Summary: Action Checklist to Stay Safe

Daily/Weekly:

- Use only business accounts for real estate-related purchases
- Monitor credit card due dates
- Categorize new expenses in your accounting software

Monthly:

- Review credit reports and utilization
- Reconcile bank and credit card statements
- Evaluate whether any credit lines need to be repaid or increased

Quarterly:

- Review legal compliance (LLC renewal, filings)
- Meet with CPA or bookkeeper to review tax planning
- Submit updated income docs to lenders if needed

Annually:

- File taxes with all credit-related deductions properly documented
- Review and update business registration, website, licenses
- Evaluate your entire credit stack for optimization or consolidation

Coming Up Next...

Now that you know how to avoid costly credit and legal mistakes, you're ready for the next stage: designing your **long-term exit strategy** and building generational wealth. In the next chapter, we'll dive into refinancing, equity plays, and what to do once you've built your portfolio using business credit.

Let's start planning your freedom.

Chapter 9: Exit Strategies and Building Long-Term Wealth

Once you've used business credit to acquire and stabilize multiple properties, the next phase isn't just maintaining what you've built—it's using smart exit strategies to multiply your wealth.

In this chapter, we'll cover:

1. Why exit strategies matter—even if you never plan to sell
2. Refinancing and equity harvesting
3. Selling with maximum profit and tax efficiency
4. Leveraging your portfolio for wealth and credit expansion
5. Building a long-term plan for financial independence

Step 1: Understand Why Exit Strategies Are Essential

An **exit strategy** isn't just about selling—it's about knowing when, why, and how to reposition your capital for the next opportunity.

Without a clear exit plan:

- You may miss out on market timing opportunities

- You might overleverage or underutilize your equity
- Your credit lines may stay tied up longer than necessary
- You could face high taxes, lost profits, or poor cash flow

Common Real Estate Exit Strategies:

- **Refinance and hold** (long-term cash flow, equity harvesting)
- **Sell for profit** (at market peak or post-renovation)
- **Cash-out refinance** (extract equity for new deals)
- **1031 exchange** (defer taxes by trading up)
- **Seller financing or lease options** (creative exit structures)

Step 2: Refinance to Free Up Credit and Expand

One of the most powerful exit moves is **refinancing your real estate through a DSCR lender** or business-friendly bank to pay off initial credit lines and reposition the property for the long-term.

How to Structure a Refinance:

- Wait 6–12 months post-acquisition to show property income and stability
- Work with your existing DSCR lender or shop new ones

- Request a refinance quote based on current value and rental income
- Use proceeds to pay off business LOCs or credit cards used during acquisition

Benefits of Refinancing:

- Pay off higher-interest debt
- Free up credit for future deals
- Lock in long-term fixed-rate debt
- Potentially lower monthly payments
- Turn short-term leverage into long-term ownership

Pro Tip: Request cash-out refinance terms if the property has appreciated or been improved. Some lenders allow 75–80% LTV based on the new appraised value.

Step 3: Sell Strategically for Maximum ROI

Even if your plan is to build a rental empire, selling a property can sometimes be the best exit—especially if:

- The property has appreciated rapidly
- Market demand is high
- You want to reposition capital into a larger or more profitable asset

Steps for a Profitable Sale:

1. **Stabilize property**: Ensure occupancy, clean records, and curb appeal
2. **List with investor-savvy agents**: Especially those who understand cap rates and DSCR
3. **Minimize taxes**: Use a 1031 exchange to defer capital gains
4. **Time the market**: Sell during peak seasons or rising interest rate periods
5. **Show off cash flow**: Investors buy cash flow, not charm—highlight NOI and rent rolls

Example Exit: You purchase a fourplex using $30,000 in business credit and a DSCR mortgage. Two years later, you sell it for a $75,000 profit and pay off all business credit, then roll the gains into a larger 6-unit property.

Step 4: Leverage Your Portfolio to Multiply Credit and Wealth

The more properties you own and stabilize, the more powerful your financial profile becomes—not just in terms of cash flow, but **business credibility and lendability**.

Here's how to use that leverage:

- Use rental income history and DSCR strength to qualify for larger loans
- Request higher credit card and LOC limits based on business performance
- Create a portfolio summary to show banks and private lenders
- Use refinanced equity to fund down payments without personal savings
- Partner or syndicate deals using your established track record

Bonus Strategy: Open a holding company (e.g., Keystone Holdings, LLC) to own multiple property LLCs. This makes it easier to consolidate accounting, secure portfolio-level credit, and eventually sell or refinance multiple assets under one umbrella.

Step 5: Build a Long-Term Wealth Plan with Business Credit

You didn't start this journey just to get one or two deals done. You're building a life of freedom, control, and passive income. The final step is **turning this system into a long-term wealth machine**.

Design Your Plan:

- Determine how many doors you want to own

- Decide whether to hold forever, refinance in phases, or sell at milestones
- Use business credit not just for purchases—but for tax strategy, maintenance, marketing, and expansion
- Set annual financial goals: revenue, equity, and debt limits
- Build a team: CPA, attorney, property manager, bookkeeper, credit strategist

Legacy Building Tip: Real wealth isn't just about what you earn—it's about what you **own**, what you can **pass on**, and how you **structure it to last**.

Start small, scale responsibly, and reinvest intelligently. In 5–10 years, your real estate holdings and business credit profile can become a self-sustaining empire.

Summary Action Plan

Short-Term (0–6 months):

- Refinance one property to repay credit
- List one property for strategic sale if market timing is optimal
- Build a portfolio overview document to present to lenders

Mid-Term (6–12 months):

- Apply for higher credit limits using updated financials
- Set a goal for number of new doors to acquire
- Plan a 1031 exchange for a cash-out exit

Long-Term (1–3 years):

- Open a holding company for asset protection and tax savings
- Scale to 5–10 stabilized properties
- Build passive income to replace active work
- Consider estate planning, trusts, or private lending

Coming Up Next...

In the final chapter, we'll help you map out a **90-day action plan** that ties everything together—from building your foundation to closing your first (or next) business-credit-backed real estate deal.

Let's turn your knowledge into motion and your credit into capital.

Chapter 10: Your 90-Day Action Plan

You now have the complete blueprint for leveraging business credit to fund real estate deals—from structuring your business and building credit to acquiring and scaling properties. But none of it matters without execution.

This chapter gives you a clear, practical **90-day roadmap** to take action. Whether you're starting from scratch or optimizing an existing business, this plan helps you move forward with speed and clarity—using the exact steps outlined throughout this book.

What You'll Accomplish in 90 Days:

- Build or optimize your fundable business structure
- Establish strong business credit with vendor and tradeline accounts
- Get approved for business credit cards and lines of credit
- Fund and close your first—or next—real estate deal
- Prepare to scale with confidence and consistency

Phase 1: Week 1–4 | Foundation Building

Primary Goal: Set up your business entity and fundability profile.

Tasks:

1. **Form a Legal Entity**
   - Register your LLC or corporation with your state
   - Obtain your EIN from the IRS
   - Apply for a business license if required in your locality
2. **Establish a Professional Business Presence**
   - Set up a dedicated business phone number
   - Purchase a professional domain and email (e.g., info@yourcompany.com)
   - Create a simple, clean website outlining your services and mission
   - List your business on Google, Yelp, and local directories
3. **Open Financial Accounts**
   - Business checking account with a bank that supports commercial credit
   - Consider digital banks that integrate with credit apps (e.g., BlueVine, Mercury)
   - Open a basic accounting software account (QuickBooks, Wave, Xero)

4. **Apply for a D-U-N-S Number**
    - Go to dnb.com and apply for your free number
    - Ensure your business info is 100% consistent across all registrations

Outcome by Week 4:

- Fully formed and fundable business entity
- Online presence established
- Financial infrastructure ready for credit applications

Phase 2: Week 5–8 | Credit Building and Access

Primary Goal: Build credit history and secure business credit products.

Tasks:

1. **Apply for Tier 1 Net-30 Vendor Accounts**
    - Choose 3–5 vendors (Uline, Quill, Grainger, Summa, Nav)
    - Place small orders ($50–$100) and pay within 10–15 days
    - Track due dates and follow up to confirm reporting
2. **Set Up Business Credit Monitoring**

- Use Nav.com or CreditSignal for weekly score updates
- Track Paydex (D&B), Intelliscore (Experian), and Equifax Business reports

3. **Apply for Business Credit Cards**
    - Use your EIN for application (avoid PG if possible)
    - Target cards with 0% APR for 6–12 months
    - Examples: Chase Ink, Amex Blue Business Plus, Capital One Spark
4. **Apply for a Business Line of Credit (LOC)**
    - Submit financials (3–6 months bank statements)
    - Start with online lenders like BlueVine or Fundbox for faster approval

Outcome by Week 8:

- 3–5 trade lines reporting
- Business credit scores active
- $5,000–$50,000 in total business credit access

Phase 3: Week 9–12 | Deal Execution

Primary Goal: Acquire or fund your first property using business credit.

Tasks:

1. **Find a DSCR-Qualifying Property**
    - Use real estate agents, wholesalers, or MLS
    - Target properties with strong rental income and light rehab needs
    - Calculate DSCR using projected rent / PITI (aim for DSCR 1.2+)
2. **Get Pre-Approved for a DSCR Loan**
    - Choose a lender (CoreVest, Kiavi, Lima One, Visio, etc.)
    - Submit property details, rent estimates, and business docs
    - Obtain a conditional approval letter
3. **Fund Deal Costs with Business Credit**
    - Use cards for inspection, appraisal, and earnest money
    - Use LOC or working capital loan for down payment and closing costs

   - Track all expenses through your business accounts

4. **Close in Your LLC's Name**
   - Title, insurance, and deed under your business
   - Secure the property with long-term DSCR financing
   - Begin tenant placement or management onboarding

Outcome by Week 12:

- First business credit–backed deal completed
- Systems in place to manage cash flow and expenses
- Credit lines intact and ready to recycle

Bonus: Optimization Tasks (Ongoing)

To further accelerate results:

- Request credit limit increases every 90–120 days
- Apply for additional vendor accounts for diversity
- Refinance stabilized property to pay off initial credit
- Set up automated payments and tracking for all cards
- Create a repeatable checklist for your next deal

Avoid These Common 90-Day Pitfalls

- **Skipping steps:** Don't rush to funding without a complete foundation
- **Mixing personal funds:** Keep all business expenses separate
- **Overapplying:** Too many credit applications early on can hurt approval odds
- **Failing to follow up:** Confirm vendors are reporting and credit scores are updating

Your First Milestone

At the end of these 90 days, you should:

- Own a fully funded real estate deal through your business
- Have over $20,000–$100,000 in available business credit
- Be positioned to scale into your second deal within 30–60 days
- Have the confidence and knowledge to repeat this process

Final Thoughts

This action plan isn't theory—it's a playbook you can use for the rest of your investing career. Whether you buy one property a year or ten, the principles don't change. Structure smart. Build business credit. Leverage it wisely. Reinvest profit. Protect your assets.

You now have the keys. The only thing left to do is drive.

The Next 90 Days

Maya opened her notebook and turned to a fresh page. At the top, she wrote in bold: **"90-Day Plan: From Property #3 to Financial Freedom."**

She took a breath and smiled. It was the first time in years that she felt totally in control—not just of her money, but her direction.

She had used business credit to fund three properties in less than a year. No personal debt. No stress. Just systems, strategy, and one bold decision after another.

But now, it was time to go from *capable* to *unstoppable*. Time to turn momentum into mastery.

Week 1–4: Starting Again, Smarter

Maya had already created her first LLC. But this time, she wasn't setting up just a company—she was building a **real estate group**. A brand. A system.

She formed a new LLC: **Keystone Equity Holdings, LLC**. This would be her parent company. Underneath it, she planned to create a new LLC for each new property or cluster of rentals.

She registered it with the state. Got her EIN from the IRS. Set up a virtual office address in downtown Orlando. She opened a new bank account. Ordered new business cards. Her website was live within a week.

She even went a step further: she created a branded Google Business profile, set up a professional email domain, and scheduled a monthly newsletter to document her journey.

It wasn't just about making deals anymore. It was about **building a business** that could run without her.

Week 5–8: Fueling the Fire

Next came credit. Maya already had some powerful tools: her Chase Ink, Amex Blue, and a $75,000 BlueVine line of credit.

But she wasn't done.

She logged into Uline, Quill, and Grainger—her old Net-30 accounts—and placed small orders to keep the trade lines active.

Then she applied for three new vendor accounts using her new LLC.

Within two weeks, they were approved. Reporting would begin shortly. She was already rebuilding credit on a brand-new entity.

Her monitoring dashboard showed new Paydex activity. She knew it wouldn't be long before she could request larger limits.

Then came her newest tool: a **Fundbox working capital line**—approved for $20,000 within 48 hours based on her new LLC's EIN and revenue projections.

By the end of week eight, Maya had over **$130,000 in available business credit** across two entities. She was playing chess while everyone else played checkers.

Week 9–12: Closing Property #4

The email came from her broker on a rainy Monday morning:

> "Small multifamily just hit the market. Seller wants quick close. Three units, all occupied, clean inspection history. Asking $320K."

Maya ran the numbers.

Rental income: $3,200/month Estimated PITI: $2,150 DSCR: 1.49

Perfect.

She emailed CoreVest and requested a new DSCR pre-approval using her new LLC. Within two days, they issued a letter.

She wired $6,000 in earnest money from her new Fundbox line. Paid the inspection fee on her Amex. Covered the appraisal with her Chase Ink.

The closing costs and down payment—$70,000—were structured from a mix of business LOCs and reserves from her previous refinanced property.

When she closed 22 days later, it was **entirely funded by business credit and previous real estate income.**

Not one personal dollar touched the transaction.

Building Her Empire—One Quarter at a Time

By day 90, Maya had:

- A holding company
- Two active LLCs with separate banking and credit
- Four properties cash flowing
- Over $130K in business credit

- A checklist and calendar she followed like gospel

But it wasn't just about what she owned. It was about what she now *expected* of herself.

Every Friday, she reviewed her weekly numbers. Every month, she checked credit utilization and rent roll.

Every quarter, she requested credit limit increases, applied for a new line of credit, and evaluated refinance or 1031 options.

She had built a flywheel. Her business credit opened doors. Her rentals repaid the credit. Her credit grew with her cash flow. And her wealth scaled while she worked less.

The Bigger Vision

That night, Maya sat by her window as the Florida rain came down in slow waves. She flipped back to the first page of her old notebook—the one where she had scribbled goals she wasn't even sure were possible.

- Replace active income with passive? Done.
- Own five doors? She had eight.
- Build a business backed by credit, not cash? Fully operational.

But now, her vision had grown.

She wasn't just building wealth for herself. She was building something that her future family, her community, and maybe even students she hadn't met yet—could learn from.

She wrote one final line on the last page of the notebook:

> "The next 90 days won't change everything. But they will change me."

And with that, Maya closed the book, turned off the light, and rested—knowing the next chapter of her business and her life was just beginning.

Epilogue: Your Journey Is Just Beginning

Congratulations. You've just completed *How to Leverage Business Credit to Fund Real Estate Purchases*. If you've made it this far, it means you're serious—not just about funding one deal, but about building a system that can fund your future.

You've learned how to structure your business, build credit from scratch, access high-limit funding tools, and close real estate deals without using personal savings or traditional financing. That's not just a strategy—it's a new level of freedom.

But this is only one chapter in your wealth-building journey.

Other Books in the *Credit to Capital* Series

By Joe Correa

Unlock the full financial journey with these powerful and practical books in the *Credit to Capital* series. Each volume is designed to help you build, repair, and leverage credit to create wealth, purchase property, and launch businesses—no matter where you're starting from.

- **Book 1: How to Establish Credit in the U.S.**
- **Book 2: Personal Credit Repair Blueprint**
- **Book 3: How to Build Credit Fast Without Debt**
- **Book 4: Business Credit Mastery**
- **Book 5: Credit Card Secrets for Building Wealth & Rewards**
- **Book 6: Credit Card Hacking for Smart Borrowers**
- **Book 7: How to Leverage Business Credit to Fund Real Estate Purchases**
- **Book 8: Business Credit Ecosystem: Build, Stack & Automate Unlimited Funding Without Personal Risk**
- **Book 9: How to Get $1M in Credit and Keep It**
- **Book 10: Credit-Funded Wealth for Families**

www.ingramcontent.com/pod-product-compliance
Lightning Source LLC
LaVergne TN
LVHW022231200926
848481LV00006B/2224